Original title:
The Heartbeat of Christmas Joy

Author: Matthew Whitaker
ISBN HARDBACK: 978-9916-94-366-3
ISBN PAPERBACK: 978-9916-94-367-0

Whispers of Yuletide Cheer

In the corner, a cat's on the tree,
With ornaments swinging, oh dear me!
Santa's slipping, teetering with glee,
While reindeer laugh, 'Hey, drink your tea!'

Nose glows bright, Rudolph’s on strike,
He says, 'I need snacks, not just a hike!'
Elves are giggling, trying to be nice,
But all they want is some gingerbread spice!

Melodies of Frosty Mornings

Singing snowmen, voices just right,
Their noses are carrots, they dance in the night.
Frosty footprints lead to a pie,
Who took a slice? Oh my, oh my!

When penguins waddle, it’s quite the sight,
They wear little hats, looking so bright.
Snowballs thrown with glee and cheer,
But watch out! Someone's in for a smear!

Sparkling Lights of Delight

Twinkling lights on roofs up high,
A squirrel's tangled, oh what a guy!
He flicks his tail, in a flashing spree,
"Who did this?" he asks, with a puzzled plea.

The neighbors peek through frosty panes,
While Santa's stuck in a chimney, he complains,
"Next year, I swear, I'll take the stairs,"
He shimmies and shakes, lost in his cares!

The Pulse of Festive Wonder

Mistletoe placed with trouble and flair,
Alfred the dog thinks it’s all for a dare.
He jumps up high, tangling the scene,
The twist of his body, a doggo routine!

The kids are giggling, dashing about,
While Grandma’s sipping, there’s no doubt,
Eggnog’s flying, it’s a splatter show,
With laughter, warmth, and a friendly glow!

Lanterns of Hope in Longest Night

In the dark, they flicker bright,
Illuminating all in sight.
Grandma's pies are quite the treat,
But they leave us short on feet!

Kids are dancing all about,
Spinning 'til they have no doubt.
Watch out for that wayward elf,
He just sat on the shelf!

Blessings Wrapped in Cozy Sweaters.

Sweaters bulky, colors wild,
Looking like a thrift store child.
Presents shuffled 'neath the tree,
Last week's fruitcake, oh, not me!

Auntie's smiles with tinsel hair,
Pudding sticks, beware, beware!
Laughter rising, snowflakes fall,
Oops, there goes the food and all!

Joyful Echoes of Winter Nights

Echoes of joy in frosty air,
Someone’s carol sounds quite rare.
Dogs are barking, cats take flight,
Who’s that dancing in their fright?

Snowmen wobbling, hats askew,
Family warmth, we feel it too.
Mismatched socks and funky shoes,
Every corner, festive blues!

Rhythms of Holiday Laughter

Laughter bounces like a ball,
Can't keep track, we've lost it all!
Jingles jangle, spirits soar,
Who brought that fruitcake? Oh, no more!

Eggnog spills upon the floor,
Merry chaos we adore.
Each mistake, a memory made,
Wrapping joys and syrup aid!

Melodies of Mirth Beneath the Mistletoe

Under the mistletoe we stand,
Peeking at faces, not hand in hand.
My aunt’s sweet breath smells like fruitcake,
Yet that’s the kiss everyone can’t fake.

Dad slips and trips on a hidden toy,
While Grandma's knitting brings endless joy.
Laughter echoes, we dance and spin,
Christmas chaos - where do we begin?

Tinsel and Laughter in the Air

Tinsel twirls with a shake and a twist,
My cat's on the tree - oh how he insists!
Ornaments fall, they shatter with glee,
As Uncle Bob yells, 'Hey, look at me!'

Grandpa’s snoring, acting out a tune,
While the ham is dancing, would you believe it too?
We gather 'round in fits of delight,
Merry madness fills the starry night.

Radiance of Love on a Starry Night

Stars above twinkle in high glee,
As my sister spills eggnog all over me.
Mom’s cookies look great but taste like soap,
Each bite we take tests our Christmas hope.

Cousins compete for the silliest hat,
While Dad tells stories of our old cat.
Snowballs are thrown, and cheeks turn red,
Can’t feel our toes, but we love it instead!

Warmth in the Chill of December

December's chill, but we keep it light,
My brother's freeze dance is quite the sight.
With cocoa spills and marshmallow mess,
We laugh it off - it's anyone's guess!

The fire crackles, like jokes we share,
As Aunt Maureen dresses like a giant pear.
We toast to laughter, love, and cheer,
In our happy chaos, we know no fear.

The Light of Togetherness Illuminates

With twinkling lights and some cheer,
We gather round with pies and beer.
A cat in a hat, what a sight!
It swats at ornaments, oh what a fright!

Grandma's got cookies, do we dare?
The icing's all stuck in her hair.
We sip on eggnog, it's quite a mix,
Is that a gift, or her old broomsticks?

Serene Reflections on Winter's Edge

Snowflakes falling, oh, so bright,
But my nose is red, what a fright!
Building snowmen, they’re rather stout,
One fell down; we all burst out!

In the window, cocoa steams,
While outside, kids chase their dreams.
But is that a sled or the dog?
Oops! That’s a snowman in the fog!

Festivities Unfolding in Every Heart

Presents stacked, a towering sight,
Uncle Joe’s snoring, what a night!
Wrapping paper in every nook,
Mom’s hiding gifts; hey, take a look!

The turkey’s burnt; it shrieks, alas!
But laughter fills the room like glass.
We toast to mishaps, loud and bold,
Every story worth its weight in gold!

Laughter Echoing through Frosty Woods

Frosty air, we dash through trees,
Sledding down hills with utmost ease.
Wait, where's my mitten? Oh dear me!
It's stuck on the nose of a reindeer, see!

Hot chocolate spills, laughter erupts,
Snowballs fly, oh, how it disrupts!
Frosty noses and rosy cheeks,
Each snowflake dances, our joy peaks!

Whispered Joys in Cozy Corners

In comfy nooks, we find delight,
With mugs of cocoa, warm and bright.
A cat who thinks the tree's a toy,
Brings silly antics, purest joy.

Between the fluffs and twinkling lights,
We share our secrets, giggles, sights.
A knock-kneed dance to carols' cheer,
As laughter echoes, drawing near.

Nightfall's Kiss on Holiday Lights

As darkness falls, the lights do wink,
The neighbors' bulbs outshine the pink.
We stick our noses to the glass,
And watch the fumbled snowballs pass.

The reindeer on the roof take flight,
They squeak and squeal with sheer delight.
With every thud, we jump and shout,
Is Santa real? There’s only doubt!

A Journey Along the Path of Light

We wander streets with hats that glow,
Dressed like gift-wrap, what a show!
The carolers sing, but can they rhyme?
Each note a twist of silly mime.

With lights that twinkle like our cheer,
We dance through snow and holiday beer.
A stumble here, a cheerful fall,
We rise to laugh, our hearts enthrall.

Echoes of Laughter Lamenting Time

With friends we gather, wine in hand,
To reminisce of snowy land.
Each joke a jingle, light and sweet,
A quirky gift that can't be beat.

Through stories shared of past mistakes,
We laugh until our bright heart aches.
The clock ticks down, yet still we stay,
In merry moments, come what may.

Dreams of Peace on a Silent Night

In a cozy house cats snore,
While dad’s out back, tracking galore.
Mom's in the kitchen, flour on her nose,
Whisking up trouble; goodness knows!

Snowflakes fall with a giggling sound,
The dog’s wearing a hat that’s floppy and round.
Children giggle, peeking out the door,
Hoping for snowballs—not chores galore!

Ornamented Memories Hanging on the Tree

Ornaments reflect the joy of our past,
The ones from grandma, oh, they'll always last.
We hang them up with a wild delight,
And hope no one swings them too hard tonight!

Tinsel tangled on the cat's little tail,
As we sip on cocoa in a sweet, warm vale.
Each glimmering bulb holds tales to tell,
Like how Uncle Bob once danced and fell!

Cinnamon Dreams and Morning Laughter

Cinnamon rolls and laughter abound,
Mom's trying to dance, but trips on the ground.
The smell of sweet spices fills up the air,
While Grandpa's snoozing without a care.

Kids armed with laughter and whipped cream cans,
Launching their toppings like little snow plans.
“Merry Christmas!” echoes through giggles and cheers,
As we count all the days until New Year's!

Unity in Togetherness and Cheer

Gathered together, our hearts do collide,
With laughter and love, there's nothing to hide.
We play a few games, and then take a break,
To watch Aunt Edna's pie start to quake!

Wrap up the fun with songs that annoy,
Dad's off-key notes won't dampen our joy.
In this silly chaos, our spirits align,
Celebrating memories where we all intertwine!

Breezes of Gratitude and Peace

Snowmen dance in mismatched hats,
While Santa slips in furry spats.
Elves giggle as they wrap some toys,
Reindeer rustle like rowdy boys.

Cookies vanish in the night,
While kids dream of gifts so bright.
Mom's still searching for the zest,
As Dad snores through the holiday fest.

Cradled in the Spirit of the Season

Mistletoe hangs with cheeky glee,
Auntie's dance is sight to see.
Grandpa's snore shakes every wall,
While kids just chuckle, have a ball.

Laughter echoes, cups are high,
As silly jokes pass by and by.
The cat pursues the shiny strings,
While everyone just laughs and sings.

Dreams Woven in Snowflakes

Frosty cheeks and snowball fights,
Who knew cold could bring such sights?
Sledding down on crazy tubes,
Falling deep in snowy cubes.

Hot cocoa spills on furry socks,
Sound of laughter, tickle-box.
With one big splash, the snowman’s cap,
Falls off... now he can’t take a nap!

Treasures Found in Simple Moments

Pine-scented trees and tinsel strands,
The little ones make silly plans.
Whispers hush as gifts are shared,
With surprises wrapped in love and care.

Grandma guffaws, her joy so loud,
While little Timmy hides behind a crowd.
In every giggle, smiles unfold,
The best of treasures can’t be sold.

Whirlwinds of Cheer from Hearth to Heart

Jingle bells are ringing, what a fun surprise,
A cat in a Santa hat, oh my, what a guise!
Cookies left for Santa, they vanish too quick,
Now Rudolph's in the kitchen, playing chef with a trick.

Grandma’s doing salsa, with her holiday pie,
Uncle Fred is waltzing, oh me, oh my!
The lights are a flickering, what a crazy sight,
While the dog steals a present, and runs out of sight.

Snowflakes Dance to the Sound of Joy

Snowmen come alive, with a top hat and grin,
They dance in the snow, in a wintery spin.
Kids wearing mittens, throwing snowballs with cheer,
A squirrel in a scarf, crashing our snowball sphere.

Snowflakes fall softly, like feathers from space,
But one lands in my cocoa, which now has some grace.
A snow angel flops down, half graceful, half clumsy,
Lands right in the neighbor's fresh snow, oh so funny!

Cradled in Comfort, Wrapped in Wonder

Warm cups of cocoa, marshmallows afloat,
Sipping by the fire, in my favorite coat.
An elf on the mantle, with mischief in eyes,
Turns all my pajamas into silly surprise.

Grandpa tells tall tales, with a wink and a nod,
Of reindeer with hiccups, flying through the sod.
Footie pajamas squeaking as they run to the door,
Did someone say cookies? Oh, we need three more!

Twinkling Lights and Heartfelt Delights

Twinkling lights outside, and kisses beneath,
A partridge in a pear tree? No, that’s just Keith!
He wears a bright sweater, one that tickles the eye,
Looks like a Christmas tree, but oh me, oh my!

The carolers are singing, all off-key, it's true,
But their spirits are bright, and they’re dancing too!
With laughter and joy, and a warmth that will stay,
It’s all about the moments that make the day play.

Hummingbirds of Happiness in Winter's Garden

In the snow, a bird flits fast,
With a hat so small, it won't last.
Chasing flakes like tiny spies,
Spinning round in winter's guise.

Mittens flying, what a sight,
Dogs in sweaters, barking bright.
Snowmen dance with carrot noses,
While the garden dreams of roses.

Candy canes on snowball fights,
Sipping cocoa by dim lights.
Joyful laughter fills the breeze,
Hummingbirds buzz—well, if you please!

The Warmth We Share

A mug of joy, it slips and spills,
With marshmallows dancing like windmills.
Family gathers round the fire,
Every joke builds on the prior.

Grandma’s cookies—soft as fluff,
Little ones giggle, ’cause they’re tough.
Fingers sticky, faces wide,
As sugar rush becomes our guide.

Merry tunes from radio waves,
And dad’s old moves would fill us with raves.
We wave to the neighbors, quite a cheer,
With a grin that says, 'We’re glad you’re here!'

A Blink of Time

Blink and the snowman’s losing shape,
As time’s a sneaky little ape.
Mom’s asking, 'Where’s your left boot?'
While dad’s trapped in a Santa suit.

Gift-wrapping paper flies around,
A cat’s found joy—lives to confound.
Tickle fights and laughter rapture,
Every moment’s the best kind of capture.

Resolutions made too soon,
We promise to clean—then watch cartoons!
As twinkling lights begin to fade,
Memories linger, sweetly laid.

Festivals of Light and Love in the Air

Twinkling lights on every street,
Bells are jingling—oh, what a feat!
Songs of joy fill up the night,
While squirrels plot their own delight.

A feast of cookies, pies galore,
As aunties dance and tumble on the floor.
We sing off-key, but oh so loud,
As laughter blankets every crowd.

Gifts wrapped tight in endless bows,
Papa smirks, 'These don't look like prose!'
With every giggle, warmth increases,
In heart-shaped moments, joy releases.

Sugar Cookies and Sweet Serenades

Sugar cookies shaped like stars,
Decorated with sprinkles like tiny cars.
We sing with gusto, slightly flat,
While the dog hides under the mat.

Frosting fights, who will win?
Mom just sighs, 'Oh, where to begin?'
Laughter echoes against the wall,
As flour dust makes us all stall.

Out came the carolers, off-key tunes,
Practicing under the bright white moons.
With giggles and love, we all align,
In moments sweet as homemade pie divine.

Threads of Tradition: A Tapestry of Light

Grandma's fruitcake sits quite still,
A doorstop now, against her will.
Each year we sweat, and then we bake,
With marzipan, for goodness' sake!

Tinsel tangled on the tree,
A shiny mess, oh can't you see?
Lights that flicker, some just wink,
Who needs champagne when we have pink?

Joyous Spirits in Holiday Harmony

Dancing lights on the neighbor's house,
Singing carols with a squeaky mouse.
Cookies crumble, snacks run wild,
Then we blame it all on the child!

Reindeer games on snowy nights,
Sledding down with giggles and flights.
Hot cocoa spills, marshmallows too,
A cheer for fun and chocolate goo!

Hearthside Memories and Sledding Thrills

By the fire, we roast our toes,
While Uncle Fred's lost in his snows.
Old stories told with lots of cheer,
Though half of them we can’t quite hear!

Sledding down the hill with glee,
Face first, it’s better, don't you see?
Wipeouts happen, laugh out loud,
It's holiday magic that we found!

Glimmers of Hope Wrapped in Red and Green

Christmas hats for the pet parakeet,
He chirps along to every beat.
Gifts wrapped poorly, like a dream,
Each one hides a silly theme!

Mistletoe hung too high to reach,
A holiday lesson it will teach.
Laughter sparkles in the air,
With joyful chaos everywhere!

Silent Bells of Winter's Embrace

In the snow, a squirrel prances,
Stealing treats with odd glances,
Jingle bells get tangled round,
As the giggles here abound.

A snowman’s hat flies past the street,
Chased by children on tiny feet,
With every slip and every fall,
Laughter echoes, sheer joy for all.

Hot cocoa spills, a marshmallow fight,
With frosty whiskers, what a sight!
The winter chill is all but sweet,
In every heart, there's warmth to greet.

So here's to frolics, snowball play,
With jingles bright upon this day,
As laughter dances through the night,
Winter's joy is pure delight.

Echoes of Yuletide Whispers

A cat in tinsel, oh what a mess,
Chasing shadows with pure finesse,
Each ornament, an epic quest,
While we humans just need to rest.

Mittens on hands that barely fit,
Moms in the corner trying to knit,
A gift unwrapped, a pet in glee,
What was once socks, now just a flea.

The tree leans left, not right at all,
As we gather 'round for the evening call,
With fumbles and giggles, the spirit swells,
In each other’s warmth, our laughter dwells.

So raise your glass with a hearty cheer,
This time of year brings us all near,
Through whispers soft and chuckles loud,
We celebrate together, vibrant and proud.

Frosted Dreams and Festive Flare

With frosted windows, dreams take flight,
As cookies vanish, then reappear bright,
A fairytale tale of sugar and spice,
Each frosting swirl simply too nice.

Snowflakes dance upon your nose,
While a reindeer strikes a silly pose,
With antlers made of bright red bows,
Laughter erupts, as merriment flows.

Each jingle brings a giggling fit,
As grandpa trips with holiday wit,
He shouts, "Help me, it's my big toe!"
And spills the punch, oh what a show!

In every face, there shines a grin,
As family gathers, let the fun begin,
With frosted dreams and festive cheer,
We create our joy, year after year.

Candlelight Caresses in the Snow

Candles flicker as shadows play,
While cats meow in a curious way,
Each glow reveals a happy face,
Brewing warmth in this chilly space.

The pie’s gone rogue, it jumps on the floor,
Splattered laughter, oh what a score!
With whipped cream hats and smiles quite wide,
The spirit of fun we cannot hide.

With giggles and chatter, we raise a toast,
To all the antics we love the most,
With snowflakes twirling outside our door,
We celebrate more together, and more!

So gather ‘round, let stories unfold,
In winter’s glow, our joys, we hold,
With candlelight treasures and laughter so bright,
This merry season feels just right.

Warmth in the Chill of December

In Christmas sweaters so bright,
We dance like reindeers in flight,
With cocoa cups spilling their cheer,
We laugh till we all disappear.

A snowman's hat, oh what a sight,
He stole my scarf, that little brat!
With mittens lost and toes now cold,
We chase the cat, or so I'm told.

Cookies burned, oh what a mess,
The oven's now in deep distress,
The dog just dove in, what a thrill,
Next year I vow, I'll bake with skill.

So gather 'round the fire's glow,
And tell the tales that make us know,
That laughter fills this wintry night,
And joy's the best, our pure delight.

Radiance of Embraced Moments

Under the mistletoe we sway,
But watch out! Dad's in the way,
He’s stealing kisses like a champ,
While we all just giggle and stamp.

Twinkling lights on the tree collide,
Our cat’s on duty, she’ll decide,
Which ornament makes the best toy,
A feline thief, oh what a joy!

Gift wrap battles turn into fun,
Last year’s paper? Not so done.
We’re wrapping Mom’s secret stash,
Oops! She spotted it—quick! Rush fast!

So let’s embrace these moments dear,
With silly games that bring us cheer,
For every hug and laughter loud,
This holiday makes us all so proud.

Glimmers of Hope Amid Snow

Snowflakes fall like little stars,
They dance around like tiny cars,
We try to catch them on our tongues,
But most just land on noses sprung.

A snowball fight breaks out with glee,
But Grandma aims for my big knee!
I dive behind a lovely bush,
With all my might, I make a rush.

Glimmers of hope flicker and shine,
Like tinsel hung on every pine,
But where's the light? Oh wait, it's here,
A squirrel's just stole my holiday cheer!

So let's bundle up and take a stroll,
With laughter warming every soul,
And as we trudge through winter's show,
We find the happiness in the snow.

Dancing Flames of Celebration

The fire crackles, sparks take flight,
Uncle Joe is feeling bright,
He dances near the blazing flames,
And sings out loud some silly names.

The yule log's burning with a sizzle,
We toast some marshmallows, what a drizzle!
Chocolates melt, oh what a mess,
A gooey treat, I must confess!

The dog's in pajamas, looking fab,
He snags a snack—oh what a grab!
With silly hats and holiday cheer,
We celebrate another year.

So gather close, let's share the night,
With goofy rhymes and pure delight,
Through dancing flames and hearts so warm,
This spirit's one that won't conform.

Echoes of Kindness in the Cold

In frostbitten air, a snowman winks,
With a carrot nose, he tequila drinks.
Elves on the rooftop, mischief in their eyes,
Spinning around, they dance and surprise.

Jingle bells jangle, reindeer prance by,
Santa's in trouble, his sleigh's gone awry.
Cookies forgotten, milk all gone too,
Who quenches his thirst? A raccoon, it's true!

Wrapping paper fights, a colorful mess,
A gift for the cat, now, that's just the best!
Tinsel tangled up, lights start to blink,
Laughter erupts, even Grinch starts to think.

Snowball fights rage, as laughter takes flight,
The fun doesn't stop, not even at night.
With kindness and fun, warmth fills the air,
A season of giggles, beyond compare.

A Tapestry of Laughter and Love

Gather round, folks, let the fun begin,
A grandpa's tall tale will surely win.
A story of reindeer who played the guitar,
And sang Christmas carols from afar.

Family shenanigans, who stepped on the pie?
Aunt Judy gasps, while the dog runs by.
Uncle Joe's snoring becomes the night's tune,
As we dodge wrapping paper, knees in a swoon.

Hot cocoa spills, marshmallows fly,
While cousins concoct mischief nearby.
One must not forget the dog in the hat,
A sight that's so funny, it's hard to combat.

Kindness is wrapped in a blanket of cheer,
With laughter as bright as a chandelier.
Through jokes and sweet chaos, we cherish the bond,
In moments of joy, of which we are fond.

Sweet Songs Beneath the Mistletoe

Under faux mistletoe, a cat takes a leap,
While couples all giggle, their secrets to keep.
A sudden slapstick, somebody slips,
Laughter erupts as we're fixing our grips.

Singing off-key, we take center stage,
Grandma now rapping, turning a page.
A duet with a turkey, it struts and it shakes,
Leaving us grinning, with some funny mistakes.

As the carols play, the dog joins the fun,
Chasing his tail, till he's dizzy and spun.
With love all around and giggles galore,
A season of joy, we couldn't ask for more.

Sweet songs echo out, from our hearts they flow,
In silly moments, our spirits will glow.
With laughter so sweet, like candy canes spun,
Beneath the bright twinkles, we all are as one.

The Whisper of Family Gatherings

A family affair, with dishes galore,
Who's hiding the stuffing? Oh, there's a score!
Everyone's laughing, as we share tales grand,
Mom's dancing the polka with a turkey in hand.

Grandpa at the table, he'll share a wise line,
Then forget what he said, still, it's perfectly fine.
Kids throwing crayons, the artwork is bold,
A masterpiece made, a sight to behold.

With board games laid out, the battle begins,
As uncles argue rules, oh, where to begin?
The chips get devoured, the punch bowl runs dry,
Yet laughter keeps ringing, from the low to the high.

Amidst all the chaos, a hug just feels right,
In each heart, a glow, a warming delight.
Cherishing moments, with memories bright,
In family's embrace, we find pure delight.

Golden Moments in Silver Time

In the kitchen, chaos reigns,
With flour flying like snow in veins.
Uncles dance like they're in a trance,
While grandma's eyes twinkle in a glance.

The cat's on the tree, what a sight!
Presents topple in a jovial fight.
Silly ties worn by folks who don't care,
Amidst laughter and jokes that float in the air.

Each cookie's a monster, quite lopsided,
But the taste, oh my, it can't be divided!
With gingerbread men that start to sprint,
And Aunt May's fruitcake, the ultimate hint.

So raise your glass, let the cheer unwind,
To silly memories, leave worries behind.
In this silver time, with giggles so bold,
We capture golden moments, a joy to behold.

Sun-kissed Joys of the Season

Carols sung off-key, a quirky tune,
With kids running wild under the full moon.
Imaginary snowballs thrown with delight,
While Dad's wearing Rudolph's nose this night.

The tree's all tangled in lights and fate,
Swearing the cat won't have a date.
Sharing stories, each one a surprise,
While Grandma rolls her eyes and sighs.

With mugs of cocoa that spill on the floor,
Laughter erupts, who could ask for more?
The sun-kissed warmth fills hearts with cheer,
As we toast marshmallows, and sip winter beer.

So let's eat cookies and dance like we're mad,
For these joyful times, oh boy, they're rad!
In this festive season, let spirits soar high,
With smiles and giggles that never run dry.

Soft Murmurs of Holiday Traditions

Stockings hang low, filled with odd stuff,
Like rubber ducks and socks that are rough.
Great Uncle Joe, with tales to unfold,
Makes us all laugh, his stories retold.

In the corner, a tree that leans like a ship,
Adorned with ornaments that do a flip.
Baking cookies that somehow explode,
Kitchen mayhem becomes our abode.

The jingling bells of ridiculous hats,
As cousins join in with highlight spats.
Each family photo, a hilarious sight,
With wigs and props, we suppress delight.

So gather around the warm fire glow,
With hot cocoa flung like a snowball throw.
These soft murmurs bring grins in reply,
Traditions so funny, they'll never say bye.

Crimson Hues of Love's Embrace

Mismatched mittens keep hands warm and snug,
As we cozy up tight, all cheerful and bugged.
With stories of yore that make eyebrows arch,
Riding the waves of laughter, let’s launch!

The dog peeks out from a basket of bliss,
Covered in tinsel, he looks quite amiss.
Joyful chaos fills each nook and each cranny,
As we play charades with Aunt Sally’s nanny.

With crimson ribbons tied on each treat,
And Dad in the kitchen, still stepping on feet.
Sister’s prank on the elf with a shovel,
It's all in good fun, just more laughter to revel.

So let’s sprinkle cheer, like glitter in air,
In this warm embrace, we’ve no room for despair.
In every blunder and joy, we find grace,
Amid crimson hues, love finds its place.

The Glow of Unity Among Friends

In a cozy nook we gather near,
With mugs of cocoa, full of cheer.
The sweater's tight, the hat's too bright,
We laugh and tease, oh what a sight!

Cookies crumbling on the floor,
Our giggles echo, can't take much more.
A gift wrapped strange—what could it be?
Oh, it's just socks! Not irony-free!

Toasting marshmallows, flames take flight,
We dance around, it's pure delight.
Our playlist's weird, yet we sing loud,
In our jammies, feeling proud!

Beneath the stars, a snowman sighs,
His carrot nose is not quite wise.
We give him arms, so he can wave,
To all our friends, our hearts so brave!

Tides of Joy on Frosted Shores

On frosty sands we build with glee,
A snowman's hat is stuck on me!
With frozen toes, we dash and race,
You tripped, and fell—now what a face!

The beach ball's gone, let's use a flake,
Oh, dodging snowballs is no mistake!
Our laughter rolls like waves at sea,
As the tide whispers, 'Play with me!'

Seagulls swoop, but won't steal our fries,
We guard our snacks, we won't disguise.
Around the dunes, we dance and cheer,
While family snaps us, never clear!

With glasses fogged, we push and shove,
The beach is cold, but we're full of love.
Riding waves of giggles galore,
We'll cherish this, forevermore!

Embracing the Silence of the Season

In the stillness, the world feels strange,
A cat sleeps through the “silent” change.
The fridge hums loud, my socks are wet,
I think this snow’s my biggest threat!

We tiptoe 'round the creaky floor,
While jingle bells make spirits soar.
A grandpa snores, and tot falls down,
We're tiptoeing through the sleepy town.

Hot stew's the plan, but I must confess,
Cooking is not my greatest success.
The pot boiled over, what a mess!
It might just win the culinary stress!

Crickets chirp, the stars all wink,
While we all laugh and eat, then think.
If the silence brings a little clatter,
Then let’s embrace the joyful chatter!

Nurtured Bonds Beneath the Stars

Under the glow of twinkling light,
We've shared our secrets, our hearts feel light.
With mugs held high, to silly dreams,
A toast to all our wild extremes!

Just look at Dave, he's lost his hat,
He's searching through the nearest cat!
We roll with laughter, arms open wide,
As memories dance, we cannot hide.

The warmth of pals, it fills the space,
In mismatched sweaters, we embrace grace.
The trees sway gently, swaying too,
To beats that only we all knew!

As stars align, our giggles soar,
With silly gifts, we always want more.
For in this night, our hearts are free,
Beneath the stars, just you and me!

Whispers of Gratitude Across the Table

Families gather, the turkey's a sight,
But Uncle Joe's joke? Oh, what a fright!
A cousin is sneezing, the pie's on his face,
We laugh till we're crying, what a warm place.

The table is full, but the chairs are all stuck,
Someone's eating ice cream, oh what rotten luck!
A toast with our cups, they clink with a cheer,
To awkward old stories that we hold so dear.

Grandma's in the kitchen, with flour in her hair,
While someone is hiding their veggies with care.
The laughter resounds, and the glasses all clink,
For silly tradition, we never will rethink.

As the clock ticks away, we dance and we prance,
Who knew that such chaos could lead to romance?
With whispers of joy, our hearts feel so light,
In this crazy family, everything's right.

Pine-Scented Wishes Under the Moon

The tree is a beacon, all twinkly and bright,
But the cat's in the branches, oh what a sight!
With ribbons and tinsel, the chaos unfolds,
Who needs silent nights when you've got such bolds?

Outside the snow falls, it's merry and fun,
But Aunt Mabel's sweater? No, that's not the one!
With pine-scented wishes, we toss out the gloom,
As laughter erupts in our festive little room.

The cocoa is flowing, with marshmallows afloat,
But Timmy just spilled it—oh dear, look at that coat!
We huddle and giggle under blankets of fluff,
This holiday season, my dear, is enough!

Under the moonlight, we dance and we sway,
With mischievous spirits, we giggle away.
For memories made in this festive cocoon,
Will last a lifetime, our hearts all attune.

A Symphony of Smiles and Soft Embraces

The children are squealing, the presents abound,
But Dad's stuck in boxes, oh how he's aound!
With bows and with giggles, the joy starts to rise,
As Grandma's sweet cookies bring sparkles to eyes.

The fireplace crackles, it's warm and it glows,
Yet Cousin Bob's snoring? Everyone knows!
We dance to the music, our hearts feel the beat,
While snowflakes are falling, it's all quite a treat.

A symphony plays, with some clashing of plates,
As we sing off-key, yet it only elates.
With soft embraces, we cherish our crew,
Bringing laughter and love, oh how we grew!

As moments embrace us, we savor this cheer,
Each smile like a gift that we hold very dear.
With hearts all entwined in this cheerful charade,
We toast to each other and the fun we've made.

Ephemeral Moments Traced in Glow

With candles a-glimmering, the mood starts to sway,
But the cat knocked them over, oh dear, what dismay!
With laughter and chaos, we savor each bite,
As our funny traditions make everything bright.

The cold winter air makes us race to the door,
Where snowball fights spring up—who knew there's a score?
With hats that are crooked and gloves shed away,
We revel in frolics that never will fray.

Every twinkling light tells a story so true,
Yet Grandma's misplaced her own shoe, oh who knew?
The joy is contagious; we dance without care,
In ephemeral moments, there's magic to share.

So raise up your glass to this wild holiday,
With giggles and cheers, let's laugh all the way.
For in this sweet chaos, we know that we're blessed,
With love overflowing, we're truly the best!

Carols of Friendship and Kindness

In the kitchen, mistletoe's bright,
Cookies are flying left and right.
Laughter echoes, flour on my nose,
Who knew baking could come with woes?

Friends in pajamas, hats askew,
Singing loud like it's the thing to do.
Pies on the table, one dog in the way,
'You're on the naughty list!' I hear someone say.

Dashing through sleet, half-snow in my boot,
Exchange of gifts with a neighborly hoot.
Giggles burst forth like joy in a song,
With each joke shared, how could we go wrong?

A trip to the mall, a search for a toy,
Found a sweater instead, oh what joy!
With our quirks and quirks, we'll ring in the cheer,
It's us against the world, let's make this clear!

Radiant Spirits in Shared Glances

Sparkly lights adorn every house,
I trip on the cat, as quiet as a mouse.
We toast hot cocoa, marshmallows afloat,
Each sip is a giggle, life's little joke.

Friends gather closely, all in a row,
Sharing wild tales we can't quite outgrow.
My aunt's secret recipe for a pie,
Ends in laughter as it just flops, oh my!

Laughter erupts when the camera clicks,
The tree in the back? A storage fix!
Our traditions are odd, but we hold them tight,
Comical memories make spirits so bright.

We clink our glasses, and cheer with glee,
For the magic of friendship, and you and me.
Every mishap makes our bonds even stronger,
In a humor-filled fest, we can't help but wander!

A Journey through Joyous Memories

A sleigh ride with friends, we all squeeze in,
Laughter erupts as we jostle and spin.
A snowball fight breaks, it's total delight,
Yet somehow I'm tagged, what a snow-gathering sight!

Holiday cards, a time for a cheer,
Mostly for chuckles, let's be crystal clear.
We scribble our greetings, with ink that smears,
Look out, dear postman, it's this time of year!

Pine-scented candles light up our night,
While trying to cook, we laugh in delight.
A casserole burnt? It's just part of the fun,
Who needs a feast? We'll laugh till we're done!

Under the stars, we send off our wishes,
With giggles and glee, not lavish dishes.
A toast to the moments that bring us together,
Come rain, shine, or snow, we'll brave any weather!

Sweet Emotions in Holiday Colors

Red ribbons and laughter entwined in a twist,
Pine needles falling, but what's that? A mist!
We dance in our socks on the slippery floor,
Who knew the holidays could lead to such lore?

A garland mishap, a hole in the wall,
As we hang ornaments, I rise—and I fall.
But friendship's the glue, to all of our quirks,
With giggles galore, that's how joy works!

Colorful sweaters, there's warmth all around,
"Who wore it best?" echoes out with a sound.
We twirl up the cheer, like a holiday swirl,
With joy in our hearts, we give life a whirl!

So here's to the colors of laughter and light,
With each little moment, our hearts will ignite.
As we share in this chaos, our souls do rejoice,
In a dazzling holiday, let's all find our voice!

Sweets and Treats of Joyful Celebration

Cookies stacked up to the sky,
With icing that makes us all sigh.
Gumdrops dance on every plate,
While fudge waits, we can't be late.

Lollipops twirl in the air,
As gingerbread men start to stare.
Chocolate rivers flowing wide,
Bringing sweet dreams along for the ride.

Candy canes start to break dance,
While we munch without a chance.
A parade of treats on display,
Who knew dessert could play this way?

When cake pops wear tiny hats,
And pie has thoughts like chubby cats.
Every bite a joy-filled thrill,
In this season, we feast at will!

Glowing Hearts of Shared Blessings

Lights twinkle on roofs up high,
While snowmen sip cocoa nearby.
Elves are busy, what a show,
With wrapping paper tossed in a row.

We hang stockings with silly glee,
Where each gift's as strange as can be.
A sweater that's two sizes too small,
Gifts that make us giggle and sprawl.

Neighbors share cookies and cheer,
While carolers sing without fear.
Each note's a burst of delight,
As laughter fills the frosty night.

With every joke and merry jest,
We find the warmth that feels the best.
In the joy of sharing we find,
That laughter's the gift that entwines.

A Season of Kind Hearts and Open Doors

Mittens are lost, but spirits are won,
As we laugh in the glow of the sun.
Neighbors stop by with pies galore,
A sprinkle of kindness, an open door.

With every hug and grin on display,
We dance through the halls, come what may.
Kids in pajamas do pirouettes,
While cats eye the tinsel in debts.

Chairs pulled close for stories grand,
We share silly tales, hand in hand.
With cocoa spills on every floor,
We gather together wanting more.

In the warmth of laughter, our hearts do soar,
With kind deeds waiting just outside the door.
So come one, come all, to our cheerful place,
Where love and laughter find their space!

Moments of Stillness and Warm Remembrance

Amid the calm of winter's hush,
We unwrap memories with a rush.
Cocoa sips lead to giggles shared,
As we think of the days when we cared.

The clock ticks softly, a vintage chime,
Recalling sweeps of joyful rhyme.
A time when socks were mismatched and bold,
And stories of epic snowball fights retold.

Amid the glow, we reminisce bright,
Of silly antics that brought pure delight.
With family close and laughter near,
We celebrate love with every cheer.

In quiet moments, the heart finds rest,
Recalling those times that felt like the best.
So gather 'round, let laughter chime,
As we toast to memories, one verse at a time.

Heartstrings in Twilight's Glow

In the kitchen, chaos reigns,
Cookies burn and laughter trains.
A cat steals ham, oh what a sight,
We chase it down, what a delight.

Grandma's hat, askew on head,
She cracks a joke, it's widely spread.
Spaghetti strings hang from the tree,
Don't tell the kids, let them just see.

Laughter echoes as we sing,
Off-key notes, oh what fun they bring.
Uncle Fred dances with great flair,
Knocking over the seating chair.

So here we cheer, with humor bright,
Thankful for joy that feels just right.
In twilight's glow, with hearts aglow,
We munch and giggle, love in tow.

Tinsels of Love and Unity

The stockings hang with tufts of fluff,
Yet somehow, they're never enough.
Little hands reach, eyes all aglow,
For candy canes and gumdrops to throw.

A wild dog bounds through the snow,
Paw prints on the cards, oh no, oh no!
We dress him up in tinsel bright,
He wiggles free, what a funny sight!

A snowman made of soggy socks,
With carrot nose and silly frocks.
We gather 'round, throw snowballs wide,
Giggles erupt, we take it in stride.

Families unite, with laughter and cheer,
In this hot mess, love draws us near.
Tinsels of joy shine through the night,
In every mishap, we find delight.

Cherished Memories in the Frost

Frosty mornings, sleds on the hill,
Brother flies down, brings quite the thrill.
Landing face-first in a snowbank cold,
Laughter erupts, embers of old.

Mom's fruitcake, we dare to eat,
A mystery slice, unexpected treat.
Candles flicker, shadows in play,
As we swap tales of the silly day.

A cousin's beard made of whipped cream,
The dog's not pleased, let out a scream.
Yet amidst the jokes and playful jabs,
We gather tighter, sharing our grabs.

In frosty air, our hearts take flight,
Laughter lingers, a pure delight.
Memories forged, in snowflakes spun,
Together we find, we all are one.

Embracing Magic Beneath the Stars

Twinkling lights dance on the street,
A grand parade of gingerbread treat.
Elves in pajamas with mismatched socks,
Chasing snowflakes like silly hawks.

A grandma's story, wacky and wild,
Of frost-bit toes and a runaway child.
Under the stars, our laughter rings,
Who knew chaos could spark such things?

The dog in reindeer, what a sight,
Chasing his tail in pure delight.
Wearing a scarf that's two sizes too wide,
He prances around, so full of pride.

As we embrace, under light's soft glow,
We cherish the quirks that make hearts grow.
Beneath the night's vast, sparkling vista,
We find the magic that we can't resist-a!

Gifts of the Heart Wrapped in Love

The tree is a puzzle, with lights all aglow,
My cat found a present, it's hers now you know!
With ribbons and bows, the chaos begins,
I wrapped up the toaster, oh, what a win!

Uncle Joe is a legend, he thinks he's so sly,
He swaps all the labels and laughs 'til he's dry.
A gift for my sister, it's meant for the dog,
He'll open it up, end up stuck in a fog!

Grandma's baking cookies, they're shaped like a deer,
We nibble and giggle, with laughter and cheer.
But one small mishap, she burned down the batch,
Now we're left with crumbs, oh, what a great catch!

With love all around, it's never a bore,
Even when gifts lead to "what's this?" galore.
We shrug off the mishaps, with joy we all beam,
Wrapped in the chaos, we're living the dream!

Joys of Reconnection and Reflections

Oh, family reunion, here's hugs gone awry,
Aunt Lisa's still stuck in that dance of the fly!
We laugh and we tease, as we pass the eggnog,
Dad sprinkles me with it, like I'm part of his fog!

Cousin Tim's got a story, it grows with each drink,
In the end, it's a bear, or was it a pink sink?
We gather 'round tales and relive such old pranks,
Like the time we built snowmen, then gave them all tanks!

The kids are all playing, they're wild and so spry,
Creating a ruckus, they may kiss the sky!
With tinsel in hair, they declare it a crown,
Their laughter erupts, it could conquer the town!

So here's to the moments that twist in delight,
Reconnection's a circus, but oh what a sight!
With memories like these, we embrace the good cheer,
In the chaos of love, we hold our dear sphere!

Celestial Events of Delight and Wonder

Oh, a comet's a sight, but it's grandma who flies,
With a spread of great cookies, she bakes for the guys.
In the kitchen she glows, her apron a star,
No galaxy shines quite like her, that's for sure!

The lights in the sky might twinkle and swoop,
But feel that warm glow from the spirited troop.
With giggles and dances, we moonwalk the floor,
While counting the blessings, we end up with more!

A snowman emerges, but wait, what's he doing?
He's tossing some glitter – oh no, the goo's brewing!
We dodge the bright sparkles, as laughter takes flight,
The celestial mishaps are a comical sight!

So raise up your glasses to laughter and joy,
As we hope for the magic, that's never a ploy.
In the chaos of stars, and cookies and cheer,
We spin through our holidays, year after year!

Delights Carried on the Winter Breeze

The winter breeze whispers, with laughter so sweet,
Bringing gifts that are wrapped in a snow-covered treat.
While sleds hit the slopes, faces red with delight,
We somehow lost grandma, oh boy, what a sight!

She's down by the sleds, trying out all the speeds,
While the kids holler loudly, giving her leads.
She zooms past the trees, as her wig makes a twirl,
Oh, the magic of winter, as we all laugh and whirl!

The carolers sing as they dodge all the snow,
They trip on the ice, oh my, what a show!
With voices that crack, they bring cheer to our ears,
As we join in the fun, forgetting our fears!

So cherish these moments, as breezes rush past,
With laughter and joy, let the memories last.
For winter carries whispers of joy, oh so grand,
In the wild, funny chaos, we're all hand in hand!

Flickering Candles of Togetherness

In the glow of candles bright,
We gather around, a hilarious sight.
Uncle Joe's snoring, a soft, sweet tune,
While Aunt Sue's dance moves can make us swoon.

Laughter fills the room, like gingerbread musk,
The cat’s in the tree; it’s a Christmas must.
Fruitcake is present, it’s as hard as stone,
But together we chuckle, we’re never alone.

There’s a sneak peek of gifts, all wrapped up tight,
Sneaking a peek feels just so right.
Grandma's old stories, we look and nod,
'Is that a tale or just the eggnog facade?'

As candles flicker, and laughter ignites,
The warmth of our silliness fills up the nights.
A holiday cheer like snowflakes on air,
With every little giggle, we banish despair.

Lullabies of Winter's Embrace

The snowflakes swirl, they gather and dance,
While we trip on the cookies, oh what a chance!
Hot cocoa spills, like a wintertime dream,
With marshmallows floating, it's all quite a theme.

Blankets piled high, a mountain so steep,
Dad snores like a bear; it's that time, no sleep.
Sister's got glitter, she's covered in gold,
'Tis the season for chaos, or so I'm told.

We sing off-key, it's a musical show,
While the tree toppers wobble, just watch them go!
An elf in our midst, oh what a delight,
But tripping over tinsel? A common goodnight.

With winter outside, so chilly and bright,
We find our own warmth in the comical night.
With each wacky moment, we come to proclaim,
Embracing the laughter; it's all just the same.

Joyful Revelations of Giving

Gift wrap disasters, tape flying wide,
As we swerve through the mess, what a jolly ride!
Surprises await, the excitement is strong,
While the cat takes a bow, as if he belongs.

One box is a sweater, three sizes too small,
Mom tries it on, but I can’t help but fall.
Dad’s socks on the dog? A sight to behold,
Laughter erupts, forget presents of gold!

A trip to the mall, it’s a wild, wild spree,
Elves on a break, sipping cocoa with glee.
I’m dodging the crowds, blending in line,
“Was that truly the gift?” Oh, never mind!

With hugs and with laughter, our hearts grow so light,
The finest of presents is sharing delight.
It's not just the boxes, with ribbons on top,
But the joy that we spread; it never will stop.

Nutmeg Dreams and Cinnamon Whirls

In my kitchen, oh what a sight to behold,
Flour on my face, it's a tale to be told.
Nutmeg and laughter, they swirl in the air,
Cookies are baking; we don't have a care.

Cinnamon rolls rising, they fumble and fall,
I trip on my whisk; it's a meltdown of all.
Sugar sprinkles fly, like confetti galore,
With each little mess, we just want to bake more!

Friends gather 'round with their pans and their spoons,
While singing our favorite ridiculous tunes.
A spatula battle, frosting on nose,
Such joyful pandemonium, everyone knows.

So let the ovens blast, let the laughter ignite,
With nutmeg dreams, everything feels just right.
In funny chaos, our spirits will twirl,
Creating sweet memories, oh what a whirl.

Milton Keynes UK
Ingram Content Group UK Ltd.
UKHW022010131124
451149UK00013B/1097